Our New Baby

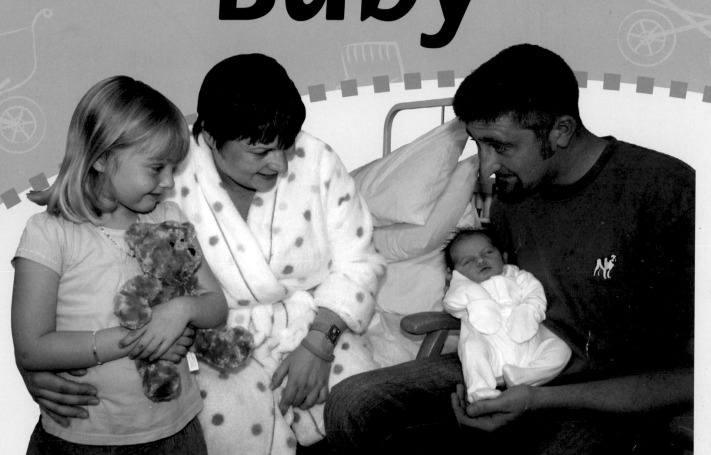

By Jillian Powell

Photography by Ruth Josey

Published in 2015 in Great Britain by Wayland

Dewey Number: 306.8'75-dc22
ISBN: 9780750294843
10 9 8 7 6 5 4 3 2 1

MIX
Paper from
responsible sources
FSC® C104740
FSC
www.fsc.org

Wayland
An imprint of
Hachette Children's Group
Part of Hodder & Stoughton
Carmelite House
50 Victoria Embankment
London EC4Y 0DZ

Editor: Julia Adams
Produced for Wayland by Discovery Books Ltd
Managing editor: Rachel Tisdale
Project editor: Colleen Ruck
Designer: Ian Winton
Photography: Ruth Josey
Consultant: Helen Beale (Teacher and Library Coordinator,
Robert Le Kyng Primary School, Swindon)

The author and photographer would like to acknowledge the
following for their help in preparing this book: Abi Matthews;
Colleen Poulton; Steve Sumner; Holly Sumner; John Polton;
Helen Hughes; M & Co; Nurses and staff at Ludlow Community
Hospital.

Printed in China

An Hachette UK Company

www.hachette.co.uk

www.hachettechildrens.co.uk

Contents

My family

My name is Abi.
I like playing in
the park with
Mum and Dad.

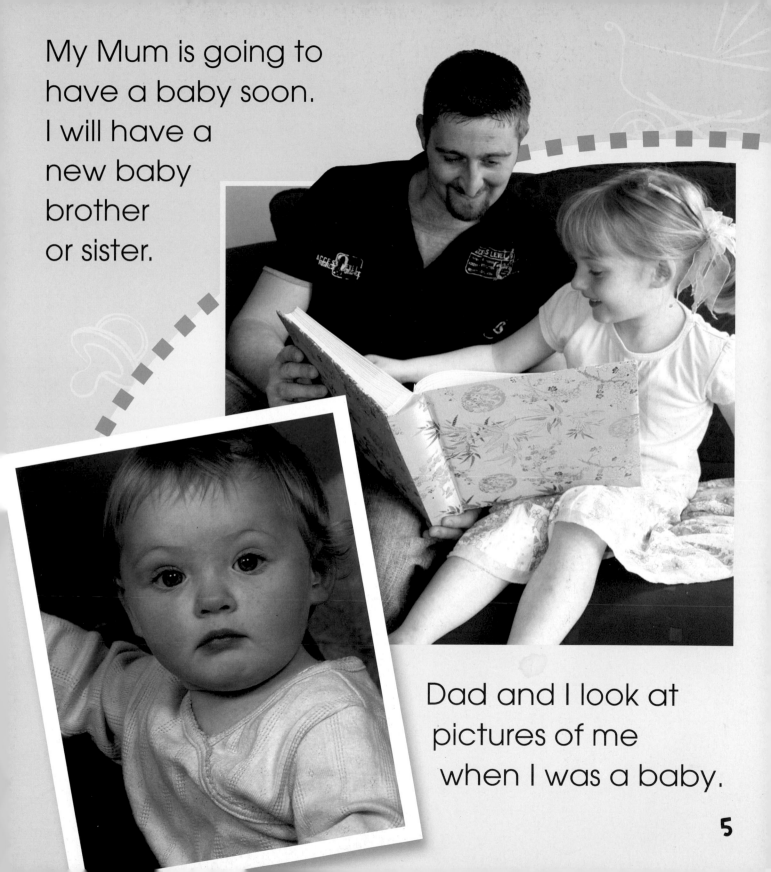

My Mum is going to have a baby soon. I will have a new baby brother or sister.

Dad and I look at pictures of me when I was a baby.

5

Shopping for baby

We are getting everything ready for the new baby.

Dad gets the **buggy** ready. It will be great when we can take the baby out in it.

I go shopping with Mum for baby clothes.
Mum wants me to help her choose.

There are so many
baby clothes. I
choose an **outfit** with
a baby bear on it.

Getting ready

Mum's tummy is getting bigger. She says she can feel the baby kicking!

If I put my head on Mum's tummy, I can feel the baby move, too.

Mum is going to **hospital** to have the baby. We are getting her bag ready.

I don't want Mum to go!

Mum says she will be home soon. I can't wait to see the baby.

Mum goes to hospital

It is time for Mum to go to hospital. Dad goes with Mum. Granddad stays to look after me. We are all very **excited**.

We get a phone call. Mum has had a
baby girl. She is called Holly. Granddad
takes me to meet her. She is so small!

My sister Holly

Mum has to stay in hospital today. She needs lots of sleep and so does Holly.

I like holding Holly's hand.

The next day Mum
and Dad bring
Holly home.

Granddad and
I are very happy
to see them.

Helping out

I want to help Mum and Dad look after Holly.

Mum shows me how to hold Holly **gently**, so she feels safe and happy.

I help Dad change Holly's **nappy**.
Holly cries when she is wet and
needs a clean nappy.

Dad shows me how
to put the nappy on.

15

At home with my sister

Holly cries to tell us when she is **hungry** or **thirsty**.

I stay very quiet while Mum gives Holly her milk.

Granddad comes to see us. He has got a **present** for Holly. There is one for me, too.

Playtime

We take Holly to the park in her **carrycot**. I show her where I play. Dad says when Holly is older she can play with me.

I like playing
with Holly on
her playmat.

Holly likes to
watch the toys.

Bath and bedtime

Holly has a bath before she goes to bed. I help Dad give Holly her bath.

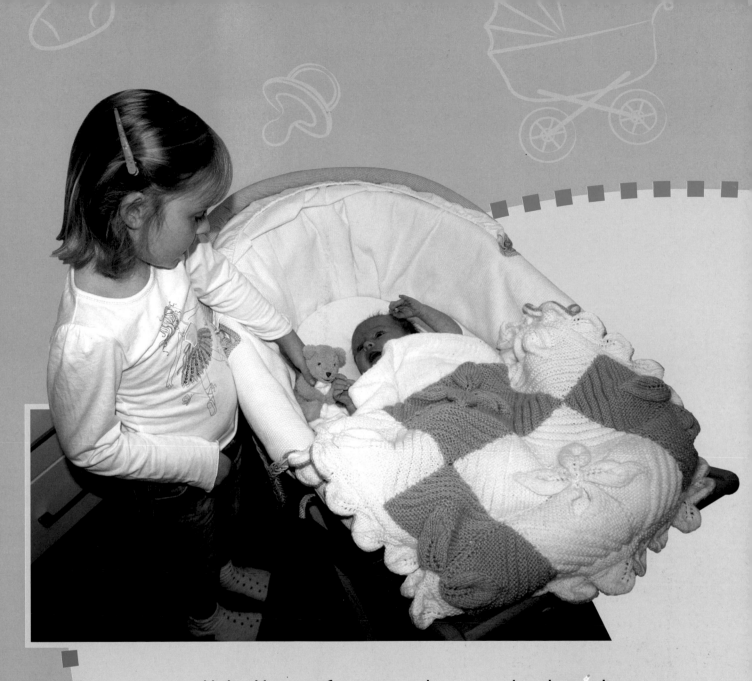

It is time for me to go to bed,
so I say goodnight to Holly.
I love my new sister!

Glossary

buggy a pushchair that folds up.

carrycot a cot that can be used to carry a baby around.

excited feeling happy and looking forward to something.

gently softly and carefully.

hospital a place where people stay when they need to be cared for by doctors and nurses.

hungry wanting food.

nappy towels that babies wear before they can use a potty or toilet.

outfit a set of clothes worn together.

present a gift from one person to another.

thirsty wanting a drink.

Further information

Books

Meet The Family: My Sister by Mary Auld (Franklin Watts, 2008)

The Big Day! A New Baby Arrives by Nicola Barber (Wayland, 2008)

People I Know: Brothers and Sisters by Leon Read (Franklin Watts, 2008)

Websites

www.bbc.co.uk/cbbc/bugbears
This interactive website provides support and advice for children facing new situations, such as what to expect when Mum has a new baby.

www.cyh.com
The Kids' Health section of this website includes helpful facts and information on health topics such as 'A new baby in the family', 'Mum's having a baby' and 'Brothers and Sisters – being the oldest'.

www.kidshealth.org/kid/feeling/home_family/new_baby.html
Offers facts and information about having a new baby in the family.

Things to do

Speaking and listening
Do you have any brothers or sisters? Take a picture to school and tell your friends and your teacher about him or her.

Music
Think of your favourite nursery rhyme. Can you sing it to your brother or sister?

Art/Speaking and listening
Make a Welcome Home banner for your new brother or sister. You will need: four pieces of A4 paper; sticky tape; paints and paintbrushes. To create the banner, stick the four pieces of A4 paper together using sticky tape. Be sure to stick the shorter sides of the pieces of paper to each other. Now write Welcome Home! across the banner. Decorate the banner using the paints. Ask an adult to hang it across or above the front door of your home. You can even take a picture to show everyone at school. What else can you do to make your new brother or sister feel welcome?

Index